"I didn't have time to write a short letter,
so I wrote a long one instead."

- Mark Twain

The Lost Art of COLD CALLING

It's a short one.

~. _ .~

The Lost Art of COLD CALLING

Turning the Tide with a Conversation

Matt Wanty

Priority House

Published by Priority House

First published in the United States of America by Priority House
This paperback edition published in 2017.

ISBN-13:
978-0692841594 (Priority House)

ISBN-10:
0692841598

Cover Photo by Rawpixel.com acquired through Shutterstock, Inc.

Printed by Amazon

Cold calling is not dead.

~. _ ,~

Dedicated to William F. Wanty

I lost my father suddenly when I was 22 years old. I've never had the opportunity to dedicate anything in his honor but this book is fitting. My dad was a general contractor and I grew up working as a carpenter for the family business. While home during the summer before my final year of college I was on a job site with my dad and oldest brother. Contemplating my future I told my dad that I didn't know if I wanted to be a salesman. He laughed and quickly replied "you'll need to get over that real quick". He said "Matt, you will always have to be a salesman because you'll always have to sell yourself". I never questioned working in sales again after that, thanks Dad. I hope you know how much you've impacted my life and how I've incredibly missed you.

Contents

1

Introduction

It could be that in this time, the year 2017, there are more sales people than ever being incorrectly taught the fundamentals of cold calling. In response, I wrote this book to help business-to-business (B2B) sales people become better cold callers. I didn't write this book to hear myself talk and hence it's not very long. Long winded isn't my favorite and I figured most sales and business people would appreciate that. I meant to only include what I thought would help sales people become better cold callers and not to mind numb readers with the same information over and over. The cold calling philosophies shared are based on my own sales experience over twenty years. There was no research done for this book and I don't recall ever reading a book on cold calling. Since the book is solely on the topic of cold calling I think it's even more important that it's well written and semi-entertaining. I truly hope you enjoy it and thanks in advance for giving it a chance.

Now, if someone went ahead and purchased this book for you, that probably means they think cold calling is an important part of your sales process. They may also feel like the sales team in general could be doing a better job of it. If you happen to be brand new to cold calling than that's perfect, I hope this book starts you off with a positive perspective of the most important aspect of your job. For those sales people reading this book who already have a generally negative or neutral experience with cold calling, don't freak out. This book could be a real chance for you to make a fresh start with the most important aspect of your job. The first thought that I would share with anyone who was given the book is this; cold calling only sucks if you're not succeeding.

Before reading a book about cold calling you'll probably want to know a little bit about the person who wrote it. I'm not a sales trainer, I will never work in corporate sales training or teaching (not that there is anything wrong with those professions). I say this because I'm a salesman, I genuinely enjoy sales and cold calling. Don't get me wrong, sales isn't the only thing I do at this stage of my career but it will always be the most important. My sales success has been mostly the result of my ability to cold call and to turn the tide with a conversation. In small part, I was taught this skill as a junior salesman but in many ways I developed it on my own through self-improvement. You can skip most of that because this book shares everything I know about cold calling and in return you have paid the price of the book. I think that's a fair deal but I also truly hope after reading about my cold calling philosophies your sales numbers sky rocket. It isn't going to happen overnight but if you want it you can get it. If this becomes the best book you've ever purchased for me it doesn't really matter because you've already paid for it. Ha, I'm totally kidding! I hope the book helps you feel better about cold calling and thus you get better doing it, which will in turn make you more money.

I've been fortunate in my career to sell a handful of million dollar plus contracts while working for a large corporation and I was able to land a flagship account for my own small business (SMB). Three of those new business sales, including the two largest, started with a single cold call to a high level decision maker. It is my experience that opening up a door with a cold call is the single greatest feat a salesperson can accomplish. It's like a grand slam in the World Series, a royal flush at the Poker Championships, like finding a Shiny in PokemonGo (couldn't leave my nerds out). It doesn't happen every day and when it does it's the most exhilarating thing you can experience in sales. Closing deals is necessary but it's usually a ton of never ending work, jumping through hoops and satisfying all the stakeholders. A new deal will often close long after the initial cold call but it would have never happened without that first important conversation. No matter the dollar value, taking a decision maker from a cold state to a place where they are actually considering doing business with your company, that's the real deal in my opinion. Sales people that can do that succeed over and over again. If you're not already a good cold caller you certainly can be, it all starts with understanding the total picture of what your company does and who you're calling and it ends with practice and confidence.

I've been cold calling throughout the last twenty years. It has always been the strength of my sales process and I also use cold calling as a research tool when I'm checking out business opportunities. It's weird for me to type these next words but there is a faction of sales people in this world that believe cold calling is dead. I guess we want them to keep thinking that. Maybe it's comfortable to think cold calling is no longer relevant because you're scared or not very good at it. Cold calling will never be dead. Cold calling is control. I decide to call you when I want to call you. I'm not waiting for a prospect to search on the internet and maybe find my company's website. I'm calling them up and making sure they know what my company can do for them. Without cold calling outbound sales would just be marketing. Maybe the sales people that are writing these long blogs about how much cold calling sucks are just in the wrong profession. Cold calling is the most important skill involved in outbound sales and neither will be dead anytime soon.

I hear and read people say that so much has changed in sales and cold calling over the last few decades. Maybe in some ways that's a fair statement because of millennials and technology. But I've also found that for me with cold calling, nothing has changed. Decision makers have always been difficult to get on the phone and maybe business leaders and sales people were more patient ten and twenty years ago. Once a sales person gets someone of importance on the phone it's still their natural reaction to try to instantly get off, that's nothing new. The fact of the matter is speaking to someone on the phone who **doesn't** want to be talking to you is hard and it always will be. But it's a really important skill if you want to have more control over your sales and business success.

In preparation for writing this book I spent the last year working as a Sales Development Representative for a fifty million dollar technology company. My job was to cold call high level decision makers at major corporations all over the country. It was my responsibility to get these decision makers or their team into a discovery meeting where we could provide more detailed information about the technology. In order to find success I had to work outside of the sales cadence that was mandated by the leaders of this company. I strongly believe and now have unfortunately been forced to witness that contacting decision makers 8 times in 15 days is a bad idea.   That's every other day, man. I think some business people today may be confusing outbound sales with something else altogether.

Contacting a Vice President at Progressive Insurance every other day for two weeks is completely insane and it's certainly not a good way to create a meaningful conversation. But, I can sadly say it's the way many technology and other companies approach outbound sales today. Why? I have no idea. My guess, in part because there are companies selling engagement tools that manage these cadences and they recommend or suggest this type of approach. Developing a technology tool that manages a sales cadence doesn't necessarily mean those people have expertise in B2B sales. If someone were to tell the people who groomed me in sales about some of cadences or approaches used today, loud laughter would be heard bellowing through the Seattle Mountains.

Later in the book I'll cover in detail my approach for getting decision makers to pick up their phone. If you're working for a company fixated on harassing people with too many touches, I felt your pain. All I can say to you is that no matter how illogical the plan, you still have to produce sales to make money. I'm pretty sure that didn't help, sorry. Ok how about this. **If you're a business leader and your company uses**

aggressive sales cadences, please read my book and reevaluate that strategy. Maybe that will help…

My experience working in sales for a technology company was much different than I expected. I think it's safe to say that many organizations in this time are being plagued because they fundamentally don't understand how to succeed with outbound sales. Impatient timelines and self-focused approaches turn decision makers off more than these business leaders could ever understand. Outbound sales is a delicate game of inches, one wrong move can put you and your company on the sidelines with a decision maker for a long time. Approaching and speaking to prospects in a respectful and consultative manner has always been the best approach. I was very fortunate to grow up in sales at a Fortune 500 air freight company where the founders were masters of outbound (direct) sales. No matter what industry you work in or where you fall in tenure, having the skill to cold call and turn the tide with a conversation will make you one of the best sales people at your company every time.

Before we begin, it's important to understand that at the start of every successful outbound sale one of two bigger picture things has occurred. The first possibility is that the sales person has contacted this company at a very good time. In this scenario the rep was fortunate enough to call this company when they were either looking to add their particular product/service or they were considering replacing a vendor in this market. In outbound sales this is what I consider to be **aligning on timing**. This could have happened with an email or voicemail, or it could have been the result of a cold conversation with someone at that company, not necessarily a decision maker. Almost any sales cadence or approach would have made this connection but it would have never happened without the luck of timing. Luck is a tough variable to measure when you're forecasting your sales pipeline.

The second and only other way a successful outbound sale can begin is through a conversation with a decision maker that eventually changes that company's plan. This can occur when the decision maker was previously unaware of the information a sales person provided to them during a cold call. The conversation led the decision maker to reevaluate and eventually conclude this new information was critical and thus has altered the company's immediate plan. This is what I call **turning the tide** and it can only be done with a successful cold call. Turning the tide with a conversation is much more about skill than luck.

2

Why Cold Calling?

The Art of Cold Calling was lost somewhere between the dot com boom and the Great Recession, I'm guessing. Technology products like CRMs and sales engagement tools that send emails for you on Thursday because some developer thinks Thursday is a good day to receive emails, could be partly to blame. Make no mistake, the best sales people in the world are still the best cold callers. Success and control go hand in hand. Armed with cold calling skills the best sales people have far more control over their livelihood than their emailing counterparts. These fearless cold calling warriors have the power to impact the timing of purchases by thrusting information on decision makers that may not have otherwise been known. Rather than waiting to align on timing, great sales people instead seek to turn the tide with a conversation.

As sales people we are the foot soldiers or warriors of our company. We're on the front lines every day fighting the battles that bring our companies new clients or prevent current customers from leaving. Our role at the company can never be overstated. A highly productive sales force for a business leader is like dream come true, while an unproductive sales group can be a complete disaster. Whether you are a new or an experienced sales person you should be very proud of your profession.

Like most people in the world, companies make plans. They decide what they want to do in the future and sometimes those plans include engaging with new vendors. This is usually the time when the company's information gatherers will Google what type of vendor they are seeking. Eventually the company's new plan becomes an inbound lead for some lucky sales representative. Now, if your company was one of those that showed up in the Google search then you might be in the mix, otherwise there is not chance in sell. Unless of course, you previously made a cold call to this company and had a conversation with a decision maker. Maybe you called this company a year or two earlier and the interaction led them to adding what you do to their plan even sooner.

A cold call allows a sales person to impact timing more than any other single form of sales communication. Voicemails, emails, LinkedIn messages, and flyers will most often only align on timing. But these other forms of communication also allow the prospect to make their own perception or judgement about your product or service. They might put you in the wrong category or they may mistake your name with another company they don't like. Any number of negative things could happen that you have no control over. A conversation with a decision maker gives you the opportunity to properly communicate what your company does and make sure they understand it correctly.

Why do some sales people avoid cold calling? The easy answer, because it's really hard to succeed. It's my opinion that cold calling is the single most difficult thing a company is asking any one employee to do on a daily basis. Not including the dangerous or lifesaving work done by medical personnel, firemen, security, electricians, construction workers, etc. It is difficult to succeed at cold calling for many reasons and one of the biggest impediments is our own physical emotions. When we get the rare opportunity to speak with a high-level decision maker, emotionally it's a lot like getting into a real fight (I guess I've been in some fights, shhh!). When the person we've been desperate to speak with finally picks up the phone our heart rate goes way up, anxiety quickly builds and our adrenaline shoots through the roof. When they answer our call it's on like Beer Pong and if you don't perform you'll NEVER get another chance. Yeah, no pressure cold calling warriors. The fact of the matter is it's a boatload of pressure and that's why most sales people don't succeed at it and eventually don't even try.

Those intense emotions we're having during a cold call are working against the very thing we need to be able to do, think fast. We think as we communicate, the easier it is for us to think the more effective our words. When you have someone on the phone giving you their best jerk face, you have no choice but to say the right thing or they'll be getting off really quick. Of course that only adds to the pressure of every cold call. If you're a sales person and you're feeling these pressures as you make cold calls each day, understand that you're in a group of cold callers called Everybody ☺. As professional sales people we all go through this as part of the learning process and continued development. Dealing with your emotions and nerves gets easier with each cold call but I'm not sure they ever really go away. At least they haven't for me.

Successful cold calls give us sales people the confidence and the blind ambition that we need to keep doing what we're doing every day. The most successful cold callers actually begin to enjoy the pressure of each conversation. If you're having trouble moving past the intense nerves and anxiety associated with cold calling, there are other ways that you can try to work yourself through that. Assuming that general cold calling practice and repetition are not making you feel more comfortable, you could try reading some other self-improvement books that I've listed at the end of the book in the section 'Other books to check out'. Also keep in mind that throughout the entire history of cold calling, there hasn't been a single fatality. I'm almost certain.

If you grew up playing basketball like I did you often heard coaches say "practice makes perfect". It's not just a sports analogy I've found it applies to almost every aspect of life. As is the case with cold calling, practice and preparation are your best friends. In a lot of ways we are preparing for the unknown as we have no idea what's waiting for us on the other end of that line. Like everything else in life the more cold calls that we have the less difficult they become for us emotionally and mentally. But they'll never be easy. As cold callers we're dealing with people who don't want to be talking to us and that will always make our jobs really hard. That's just one of the reasons sales will never be simplified.

3

Who You Gonna Call

Whether you are working in enterprise sales or selling to SMB, calling the right people is the first step toward success when cold calling. Younger or inexperienced sales representatives that are still getting comfortable talking on the phone, I would encourage you to call on all levels of an organization. Talking is good. More experienced reps that have higher earnings expectations would be best suited spending their time trying to reach the (right level) decision makers. Throughout my sales and professional career this is where I witnessed many sales representatives fail. Calling on lower levels of organizations may feel safe and comfortable, but 99% of the time if you're not talking to the ultimate decision maker you're going to lose in the end.

Leads, Foremen, Supervisors, Managers and even Directors are seemingly powerless in organizations when it comes to making decisions that involve spending. Now, I'm not saying this is 100% of the time because I've seen the opposite happen myself. Keep in mind the higher level people within an organization were at one stage of their career at a lower level. If you get lucky and catch one of these rising stars on the way up they may be able to strongly influence spending decisions. These up-and-comers likely have the ear of a higher level person who will rubber stamp what they want. There can also be situations where certain departments like Marketing or Human Resources won't have a person at the Vice President level. In this case, Sr. Directors or Sr. Managers could be the highest level person for that department and may in fact be the ultimate decision maker for the company. That doesn't mean someone from the C-level or even a Vice President can't come in an override their decision though. As sales reps it is important to understand more times than not the people in these positions cannot take us where we need to go, even if they try. There is someone above them that can override their decision at a moment's notice, thus it's always better to be talking to the person who you have identified as the ultimate decision maker. Some sales processes refer to this person as the Economic Buyer, in the book this person is referred to solely as decision maker.

Every decision maker that we call has their own motivations in their career. These people have risen to high levels within their companies because they're smart people. When it comes to their jobs and their company they know everything. They're the ultimate experts at what they do (for the most part, everybody has an Aunt or Uncle). The Vice Presidents and C-level executives at companies are looking for wins in their jobs more so than anybody else. Those wins can come in the form of new vendors with products or services that solve problems for their company. A big win for any decision maker would be bringing in a new vendor that helps their company add customers and grow.

The most successful cold calls occur when we can connect our product or service to a professional win for that decision maker. If the decision maker understands that what your company provides could be a big lift for their career, you didn't just open up a door. You may have very well closed the whole deal right there in the first interaction. By utilizing the available data on contacts from sources like LinkedIn, it's very possible to premeditate a connection between what you're selling and a professional win for the decision maker. Make sure to read the decision maker's LinkedIn profile and try to understand their job duties, goals and objectives. Once you're aware of a decision maker's motivations it will put you in a much better position to have a good conversation with that person.

Small Business (SMB)

If you're calling on a small business, less than fifty employees, it's best to go right after the owner of the company or General Manager if that's the case. Most or all financial decisions at a SMB are going to be made by the owner. SMB owners can be very difficult to reach and communicate with because of two reasons. They're either so busy it's difficult to communicate with them or they're never actually at their place of work. In the case of the latter you'll need to rely on email, marketing materials and Admins to try to get your message across. In order to effectively communicate with the SMB owner who is crazy busy, it all starts with understanding their situation.

The pressure a SMB owner can be under when it comes to meeting customer demands and satisfying employee needs can be overwhelming. Relating to a SMB owner on that level will give you a big advantage, as many sales reps are self-concerned and not at all sensitive to their circumstances. Because of the SMB owner's work load it can difficult to effectively communicate your message to someone who may be constantly pressed for time. As a result your messaging has to be really concise and it would be beneficial if you could connect on one of their biggest needs or problems.

If your product or service solves a problem that can help the SMB owner save time or money, make sure to tailor your messaging so it's communicated very clearly upfront. If you feel like they don't understand what you're trying to say, then you're probably right. It can be really difficult for anyone to absorb information when they feel pressured by time. Don't be afraid to lead off with comments like "I think we can save you money" or "I think we can help make things more efficient for you". These types of triggers can bring a busy SMB owner back into a calmer state where they're actually able to absorb your message. It can be a lonely world at the top for a SMB owner. If you can approach them in a way that lets them know you're supportive and on their side, it may help you establish a strong relationship.

Enterprise

If you're calling on enterprise then you should be calling at the Vice President level or higher. I understand for some smaller dollar transactions these decisions can be made at the Director and Manager levels but it's always best to start high and get pushed down. Whether you're trying to replace an incumbent vendor or introduce a new product or service you are best served trying to speak with the decision maker. Large corporations, medium sized businesses and even larger SMB rely on Vice Presidents to make most but not all purchasing decisions. Depending on the type of organization and the scope of the project, C-level people could be involved but they will usually rely on the Vice Presidents to interact with vendors.

Enterprise Decision Makers

I've had the opportunity in my career to sell in multiple industries and to different departments within companies. I've found that it's really important for cold calling success that we know everything we can about the people we're trying to speak with. Different titles and departments will mean different responsibilities and types of people. Following is a summary of my experience with the different decision makers that we're trying to reach every day with our cold calls.

CEO – You'd be very surprised as to how many CEOs have a direct line that goes right to them and they will actually answer. It doesn't happen often but I've spoken with a handful of CEOs in my career via cold calling and it's a thrilling ride every time. Even if you don't speak with this person your attempt to call them may garner you the audience you were seeking. Obviously CEOs have a lot of responsibilities but the biggest part of their job is to make sure the company is operating profitably and effectively into the future. There isn't any specific guide book that they use to help them do their job. They get information or intelligence from the people around them like the company's management, executive leadership and the board of directors. They probably read industry publications and stay up with current news. Business intelligence is so important to them that they may even have outside consultants keeping them abreast of what's going on in their market or the economy in general.

As sales people we can be another great resource of business intelligence for a prospect's CEO. Most CEOs are constantly looking for new ideas or knowledge that will help them stay ahead of the competition. When tailoring your messaging for CEOs try to make sure to take a consultative tone. In my personal experience I've made the most impact with CEOs by leaving them really strong voicemails that make them feel like their company could be missing out on something. If you call on a CEO don't be surprised if you get a call from a VP (maybe a little heated) trying to satisfy the CEO's questions. I often put my sights on a CEO when I feel like I have a really strong prospect and the other decision makers just aren't willing to take my call. At least someone at that company needs to know what my company could do for them, may as well be the CEO.

CFO – VP of Accounting or VP of Finance - I had the pleasure of calling on this group of people for a number of years during my time at Airborne Express. Airborne (acquired by DHL) was a Fortune 500 air freight company that competed with UPS and FedEx for expedited small package delivery. They were solely a business-to-business air carrier and the company rose up in the 90s by taking numerous enterprise clients away from the big brands. We did this by saving our customers money and there is no person at a company more excited to hear about cost savings than the CFO. CFOs, VP of Accounting, VP of Finance, these are typically accounting people and they usually aren't the most talkative at first, but don't let that dissuade you. Accounting folks think in dollars and cents and if your company has the ability to reduce their operating costs the CFO or any of the VPs below could be a great person for you to cold call. As the financial wing of the company this group of people can carry a ton of weight in purchasing decisions, especially for higher dollar transactions.

COO – VP of Operations, VP of Manufacturing, VP of Purchasing, VP of Logistics, VP of Sourcing, VP of Quality or Office Manager – COOs are responsible for making sure the company runs smoothly on a day to day basis. They could be involved in a number of different purchasing decisions and the entire purchasing department may report up to the COO. If you're selling products or services that are essential for the day to day operations of a company this may be a good person to contact. I've found the COO can be a little tougher to speak with then other C-level executives. This department will typically manage the company's RFPs or RFQs, so to be included they would have to at least know about your company. Often times at larger corporations the other departments like Marketing and Accounting will rely on the Purchasing Department to locate and screen vendors. Before even doing their own outside search, other departmental decision makers will check with the purchasing department to see if they have any approved vendors in this sector. When all else fails it is beneficial to try and make sure at least this department is aware of your product or service.

CMO - VP of Marketing, VP of Channel Marketing, VP of Consumer Marketing, or VP of Digital Marketing - This is one of the more difficult groups of people to get on the phone. Because of the mass of marketing products and vendors available the sheer number of sales people calling into marketing departments has become overwhelming. This makes our jobs as cold callers difficult but not impossible. In my time working for the technology company I primarily cold called on marketing and digital marketing decision makers. While cold calling on a narrow target market over the course of nine months, using my approach I was able to speak with over 60 Vice Presidents at major corporations. To give you some perspective I was able to connect with Vice Presidents at companies like United Healthcare, Foot Locker, Morgan Stanley, Traveler's Insurance, Lucky Brand, Emerson Electric, Web.com, American Express, Motorola, Bed Bath & Beyond and many more. It is certainly difficult to reach these marketing decision makers with a cold call but not at all impossible. In 2016, I was able to at least prove that to myself.

Decision makers in the marketing world now come in two very different forms. The traditional marketing person typically fashions a riskier hairstyle and wardrobe. These marketers are highly creative people that are most concerned with things like brand recognition and the competition. As a result, they'll be willing to pick up a cold call from a sales rep from time to time. The modern marketer couldn't be any more different. The new age marketing executive is driven way more by specific data than things like image or brand awareness. These introverts make decisions based on analytics and not traditional marketing concepts or people stuff. This type of marketer is way less likely to take our call and they would definitely prefer we send them an email loaded with stats. I guess we have to do what we have to do sales people. If you've figured out a good way to connect in a real conversation with the data driven marketer please let me know, matt@subroot.com.

CTO or CIO – Chief Architect, VP of Information Technology, VP of Development, VP of Enterprise Systems, VP of Digital - These decision makers typically come from a technical background like engineering or development. As a result they are often very technical people and they're more prone to take a conversation in that direction. If you're cold calling on this group you'll need to be able to have technical conversations and at times under duress. I've found the CIO and CTO to be two of the toughest cookies to bring off their high horse when it comes to cold calling. Also, because these are technology folks they can be one of the tougher groups to get to pick up the phone. They too would much rather receive an email loaded with information than talk with a live person. Many times you will find the voicemail message of a CTO or CIO will actually instruct sales people to send them an email. I just keep calling because what I have to say can't be conveyed in an email and they don't know that.

CSO – VP of Strategy, VP of Data - CSO as in Chief Strategy Officer, this is a growing department within corporations and even large SMB. Strategy can mean a lot of things when it comes to any specific business but this department is often responsible for continual market analysis and long term business planning. Not every company will have a high level business strategy person but if they do they can be a strong decision maker for almost any product or service. The Vice President of Strategy can be a good person to call if you're not getting any traction with your target department. This decision maker will be most interested if your product or service can help them increase revenue or improve efficiency. I've found that strategy people tend to pick up their phones for cold calls a little bit more than normal.

CRO - VP of Sales, VP of Sales Strategy, VP of Sales Enablement - This may be one of the easier decision makers to speak with for obvious reasons. Much like the other titles it can sometimes be difficult to connect with a high level sales person on the phone. Some sales VPs will be frequently traveling and others may come off as far removed from purchasing decisions. However, if your company can help their organization sell more, it's definitely a good idea to try to get the VP of Sales involved. In the end they usually get what they want, I mean c'mon they're in sales! This particular decision maker could be one of the most likely to pick up the phone because of a sales person's perseverance.

CCO - VP of Customer Service - CCO as in Chief Customer Officer, another modern title for this position is Chief Voice of Customer. The CCO/VP of Customer Service is another decision maker that may be a little easier to speak with on a cold call. They manage the company's customer relations and may be most receptive to products or services that will save them time and/or help them provide better service to their customers. I don't have a great deal of experience calling on this group so I won't be able to provide any more pertinent information, sorry.

If I missed your target decision maker I apologize. I understand there are sales people out there calling on VP of Human Resources and other high level decision makers in specialty departments. You can find a great deal more information about any of the corporate decision maker titles on the internet. It is also beneficial for you to be reading the same materials to which your target decision makers subscribe. You can easily do this by joining the groups on LinkedIn in which they belong or sign up for publications for their field. The more information that we understand about the decision makers we're cold calling the better our chances of having a good conversation.

Gatekeepers – Oh the dreaded gatekeeper, what are we to do with you. I've found that gatekeepers aren't as prevalent today as they were maybe ten and twenty years ago. Most decision makers have direct lines and instead of a dedicated admin they may share a person with other executives. Gatekeepers often have the title Executive Assistant, Administrative Assistant, Personal Assistant, but generally any person below Vice President will try to prevent you from reaching a decision maker. I'm sure you understand that a gatekeeper for your target decision maker imposes a problem. A big part of the gatekeeper's job is to make sure that people don't bother their boss. In order for sales reps to be successful with a gatekeeper we're basically asking them to fail at this aspect of their job. No matter how it shakes out it's a win lose situation. There may be sales people in the world that have found a way to use Admins to help them navigate the landscape of their prospects. More power to them, if you can get anywhere with a gatekeeper you've done a great job in my book. I've come to realize that gatekeepers are just telling us sales people what we want to hear more times than not. We can't really blame them as they have lots of sales reps calling them all biding for their boss' time.

If you're attempting to communicate a message to a decision maker through their Admin, that's a lot like sending an email or leaving a voicemail. The Admin's relay message could be missing something, interpreted wrong or for some reason may lack credibility with the decision maker. If you're intentionally calling into gatekeepers trying to schmooze them then I'm not sure that's smart calling, or maybe it is. Whatever the case it is always best to try to speak with the decision maker directly and avoid trying to communicate with them through their admins.

I'm from the old school of cold calling where I mostly try to stay away from the gatekeeper altogether. Sometimes you can successfully avoid them by calling the decision maker when they're not at work, earlier in the day before 8:30am or later after 5pm. If you're calling on a really good prospect and your only option is working through a gatekeeper, then it's always worth a shot. I've found that gatekeepers are more receptive if I'm able to mention one of their company's competitors. I'm not saying you should do that every time but the Admins might often hear their boss talking about the competition. By mentioning one of their competitors it can sometimes spark their interest as they're pretending to write down your message.

Tradeshows – Tradeshows are a great opportunity for companies to reach a mass of decision makers in a short period of time. Fish in a barrel is one way to put it.

Tradeshows are the only place I know where decision makers are actually looking to have cold conversations with prospective vendors. The goal of a conversation at a tradeshow is the exact same as a cold call. We want to make sure the decision maker understands what our company can do for them in the way we want them to see it. Participating vendors can sometimes come away disappointed with the results of a tradeshow because they didn't get enough viable leads. Paying the fees and planning are only a small part of the process. How the company's sales or other personnel perform at the actual trade show will determine the overall success. If you're an effective cold caller and your company is taking you along to a tradeshow. You better be ready to turn a lot of tides; fish in a barrel.

4

Sales Training Isn't Enough – Find a Mentor

Sales training comes in many different forms and fashions. Some companies have in-house sales trainers which are usually people that had been plucked from the sales force at some point. Other companies hire outside sales trainers to come in and train their own tactics to sell and close business. Heck, some companies are so determined to succeed with outbound sales they'll have both types of trainers. I personally believe that if it's feasible for a business in-house sales trainers are always best. Finding an outside trainer that will actually boost sales and not just moral may be difficult because they don't possess enough specific knowledge about the company and industry.

I've had the opportunity of being trained by some really good sales trainers. Trainers that had a strong understanding of the sales process and the real reasons customers did business with their company. This was because at some point in their career they had success selling the very thing they were now training others to sell. But the harsh reality for any sales person is that even the best sales trainers are only going to be able to get you so far when it comes to cold calling. Even if they have a strong grasp of all the information they are normally far removed from making calls. It can be easy for anybody to lose sight of what it's like to be under the heavy artillery fire of a cold call. Typically, the sales trainer's primary responsibilities are to teach new sales people general information about the company, the industry, the sales process, and the common objections. The scope of information that you will need to absorb in order to be a successful cold caller takes much longer than the week or two spent at sales training. The real prize information needed will often times come from somewhere else within the sales force altogether.

I grew up in sales at Fortune 500 companies where the sales groups were made up of hundreds of people. It became really simple for me early on in my career, find the best sales reps at the company and learn from them. How do you find out who is the best sales person? That's usually pretty easy, just look at the sales leader board or listen up at your weekly sales meeting. If the sales leadership seems to be talking about sales rep Dave the most, he's probably the best and you need to figure out a way to make Dave your friend.

Now, if you're thinking Dave has more important things to do and I don't know if he'd take the time to teach me, you need to think again. It all starts with really good questions. If you want to learn and you're able to ask Dave good questions, he's going to help you. We all love to talk about the things we're really good at and we all know Dave is the best sales rep at the company. He has information that he's been gathering for several years and you can skip all that and start asking him at least one question every day, hopefully more.

Keep in mind Dave has his own sales job to do so tread lightly and be helpful to the person helping you. Bring him coffee and intercept stuff that he shouldn't be dealing with. Figure out a way to get Dave on your side because you need his information to quickly become a great sales person for your company. Of course you can try to drudge it out and learn the hard way one failure at a time or you can be smart and listen up to someone who has already invented the wheel. We're all a product of our environments, choose the people you learn from and control what you become.

5

Understand Your True Value Proposition –

Master Your Product or Service

All great sales people know their product or service inside and out and that knowledge couldn't be any more important than while cold calling. Cold calls are an opportunity to share pertinent information about our companies that could turn the tide with a decision maker. If you're not a master of your product or service there is no way you will be fully prepared to do this. You have no time to think and ponder an email response or ask a coworker "what should I say?". On a cold call you have to convey the right message about your company right now before the other end of the line loses patience or senses uncertainty. It's a difficult spot but it gives us a chance, a chance to say the right things and get this company interested in doing business.

Every company in existence has their own value proposition or they wouldn't have any clients. There are some real reasons other companies are doing business with your company. As a sales person you must know your company's true value proposition and it may not be exactly the company mantra you're constantly hearing. But I guarantee you that Dave, the best sales rep at the company, knows the true value proposition inside and out. That was of course one of the biggest reasons you became his mentee.

Simply put, a true value proposition is the reason(s) your customers continue to do business with you. The 'true' part of my term comes from the reality that some companies promote a value proposition that really isn't why their clients continue to use them as a vendor. Companies can lose sight of their true value proposition because they've developed new things that are important for the future. The true value proposition is what makes your company special. It's those little things that at the end of the day the decision maker saddled with this choice must decide to choose you. For whatever reason they can't live without it or they know things won't be the same by not having your product or service.

Some business value propositions are more difficult than others to understand and subsequently communicate. It's very possible to work at a company in sales for six or twelve months before you fully grasp your company's true value proposition. Sometimes this process can take much longer and that really depends on several factors. I've completed sales trainings where the true value proposition was pounded into me and I've worked at companies where the sales trainer didn't even understand it. As sales people it doesn't really matter because someone at your company understands the true value proposition and all you have to do is find them and ask them really good questions.

Technology value propositions can be harder for some sales people and decision makers to grasp because there is a technical aspect. While working at the technology company I witnessed a sales rep that had been with the company for over four years and he never really understood the true value proposition. That can't happen. That's the equivalent of a carpenter going to work every day for four years trying to use a hammer made of marshmallows. There was no way this poor kid was ever going to succeed because he never understood the true value his company offered to customers. Even worse yet he didn't know that he didn't know and nobody was aware enough to teach it to him. I wouldn't be surprised if this is a common problem plaguing many sales organizations today.

Contrary to popular belief, it is very difficult and in some cases completely impossible to convey a true value proposition in an email or a voicemail. Sales people all over the world send detailed emails and leave long voicemails about their companies assuming the receiver is going to understand the message. Unfortunately, it's a very real possibility that the decision maker won't at all perceive the messaging in the way it was intended. Even, if it was conveyed perfectly. The decision maker's own perceptions could influence how they understand or intake the content of the email or voicemail and the message could be totally misunderstood. The more complicated your company's true value proposition the less likely emails or voicemails will ever do anything but align on timing. A conversation is really the only way to effectively communicate a true value proposition.

6

Know Who You're Calling and

Why They're Jerks.

Have you ever wondered what it was like to be on the other end of cold calls? Well, I had this experience for 10 years and I can honestly say it's the worst. As a SMB owner your contact information is available all over the internet. As a result, hundreds of eager sales representatives call promoting anything from health insurance to drinking water service. It can become so overwhelming that you decide to not to talk to any of them, send me an email you instruct the gatekeeper. Whether you're calling on a SMB owner or the Vice President of Data at Foot Locker, these decision makers are receiving a ton of calls from lots of different sales representatives.

So what makes them jerks? You mean, besides all those super eager sales people calling them all of the time. Like everyone else in the world it could just be life, they could be having problems at work or home, maybe their boss was a jerk that day. It really could be any number of things affecting this one person at this specific time. Decision makers at companies in general have a lot of life responsibility. They have important jobs so first and foremost that can be really demanding. They could also have busy lives with kids and family or other big responsibilities outside of work. There may be any number of personal and private issues that have nothing to do with you. It's important to understand you might just be the brunt of other frustrations when they pick up that phone with a super gruff "This is Rick".

Outside of personal issues these decision makers may view cold calls as just simply more work. You may not realize it but whatever it is that we're calling about as sales people, it is guaranteed to cause the decision maker more work and possible strife. We're all human and none of us are too crazy about adding to our workloads even if there's a long term reason to do so.

These decision makers have also had their fair share of terrible conversations with sales reps. In the ten years running a SMB I would say that I spoke to around 20 sales reps on cold calls. The business was a simple specialty printing business so we didn't have the need for a lot of vendors. That didn't limit the number of people calling on me though. Four water suppliers, three garbage services, dozens of SEO agencies, five different ink suppliers, ten insurance reps, and lots of other random services all trying to be heard. I too had my fair share of awful interactions with sales reps during cold calls. In one case I remember a rep being incapable of understanding that his service didn't legitimately fit my business. Begging or groveling is not professional sales, sometimes we have to concede based on logic. I also remember a massive failure for a rep who finally reached me after months of pursuit. I picked up the phone and gave him my best gruff, "this is Matt". He choked, it was really bad. He couldn't get over the fact that I answered the phone and he just kept saying "so this is Matt Wanty". Very bothered by this I didn't really understand what he was selling and I never heard from him again. He had a real chance to sell me something but he wasn't ready. In my opinion he did everything right until I answered the phone. What happened to that poor sales rep can surely happen to any of us but this type of opportunity for sales people only comes so often. You have to be ready.

We all know that decision makers are going to give us their best jerk voice when they answer our cold calls. Being on the other side of the coin as a SMB owner I learned a lot about why decision makers treat sales people like this. The fact of the matter is they don't want to be answering the phone and that's the biggest reason they answer like they have the worst hangover ever. If you could imagine feeling all the torment of a trip to the dentist wrapped up in a single moment before you pick up the phone. That's pretty much what it's like for business people who are answering a cold call. Most decision makers are grudgingly aware that by avoiding calls from sales people in a way they're not doing their job. As leaders at their company it is their responsibility to make sure the company is aware of vendor options and new products or services in their market. However, these conversations with sales reps can be absolutely brutal. This internal debate of should I pick it up, should I skip this call can also lead to the initial cold call grumpiness that we all encounter.

Here's the deal, this decision maker is probably a pretty cool and down to Earth person. They're likely not the jerk they're making themselves out to be. They made it to this position at their company because they're smart and they know how to deal with people. You're a professional sales rep and you know how to deal with people too. On cold calls we always need to understand this person is not the captain hard ass they're making themselves out to be right now. In order for us to be successful in a conversation we have to get the decision maker to start speaking and acting in their normal tone. I've found that the best way to handle this grumpy person in this moment is really simple, kill them with kindness. This old school tactic will work in this situation almost every single time. It's really hard, and I can say with extreme personal experience, it's nearly impossible to continue being a jerk when the person on the other end of the phone is speaking to you in a kind manner. When this mean vs. nice dynamic is happening at a point in the conversation most decision makers almost feel a little bad. It dawns on them that they're being really mean to someone who is only being nice and trying to do their job. Kill them with kindness and it will work almost every time at bringing decision makers out of a standoffish position.

Most of us don't know that as sales professionals we can come across as really selfish people. When calling into decision makers we can seem disrespectful to their time and only concerned with our own needs. It is important to be aware that they could have a lot of things going on at the moment that are way more important to them than our product or service. We're calling these decision makers based on our time frame without any regard for their life and what's going on in their world. For example, say the Vice President of Marketing at Nautilus is under a tight dead-line from the C-level to produce a new marketing campaign with in the next three weeks. The last marketing campaign didn't go so well so this VP is feeling a little heat to make sure this one is extra special. This is a common reality for these types of decision makers in the corporate world. If you're following a sales cadence that guides you to contact this Vice President of Marketing eight times over the next few weeks, you're going to come off like a desperate spaz because this decision maker is already under the gun and probably stressed out. During your impatient two week pursuit every time they get a glimpse of one of your emails or voicemails or LinkedIn messages they cringe. Because of bad timing and impatience you've essentially debranded (I know that's not a word) your company with this decision maker. This is one of many reasons why aggressive cadences are counterproductive to our sales efforts and the decision makers that we're calling on every day.

7

Prospecting with Precision

I hope you didn't buy this book for the chapter on prospecting. A long book written about prospecting seems pretty fanatical to me. It's not that my ideas about prospecting aren't good, it's because as outbound sales people we're pretty much all in the same boat. What I mean is that the lead lists available to me are also available to everyone else. Now, how you comb those lead lists may need some improvement and that's why I wrote this short chapter.

Throughout my sales career I've always been able to find great prospects that for some reason the company I was working for had never come across. During my most recent experience in technology sales I found more than normal but that was understandable. The company only had a handful of sales people and the market was only in the early stages of maturity. But for the two Fortune 500 companies in highly mature markets, that always seemed a little strange to me. It wasn't like I was using different lead sources. Twenty years ago when I first started my sales career we all used the region's Business Journal and other similar publications. Today we all have the entire internet to scour and there are also services like Avention and HubSpot that provide detailed information on businesses and contacts all across the world. So what's my secret? Well, you did buy the book. It's really simple, I might have oversold it. Here it is, when prospecting through lead lists make sure you research **every single company** listed.

Don't skip a single line item. This is really important because our own perceptions cause us to skip over companies as we're researching lists. I found that even when I was making a point to not do it, I would still catch myself skipping over companies. I would skip them because I didn't think the name matched a company that would be in the market for what I sold. Of course that makes no sense. For example, say that we're selling parts and supplies for printing equipment. While combing through a prospecting list we come to a company called Wilson Holdings. Some of us might skip right over that name because we can't automatically assign it a type of business or industry. It wasn't like it said Wilson Printing or Wilson Publishing. We passed it over only to later realize Wilson Holdings is actually six different printing companies all of which need our parts. The point I'm trying to make is don't judge a company by the name. Decide you're going to research it no matter what because it's on your prospecting list. The second largest sale of my career was a great example of this, a company called Proficiency Testing Service located in Brownsville, TX owned by the Serafy family. Over a decade Proficiency spent millions of dollars a year on air freight and I was (happily) the first person from my 50 year old multi-billion dollar company to ever call them up. This is why it's really important to prospect with precision and research every company, follow up on every lead, kick all tires, turn over every stone. Ok I'm done, sorry.

8

Cold Call Preparation and Sessions

We live in a time where business intelligence is posted all over the internet on websites and blogs. Valuable information is readily available for any sales person to consume and use to their advantage. Understanding the total picture of every prospect will help you to be more successful on cold calls. Total picture means exactly that, anything and everything about them. Before we even pick up the phone we want to know the prospect's current state of business, current news & events, how our product or service aligns with their business, contact tree & hierarchy, and any decision maker motivations that we can use to our advantage.

A general internet search on the company will let you know any big recent events or other pertinent information. LinkedIn is a great resource for information on decision makers and I also use services like data.com in order to get free direct phone numbers. Anything that you can find out about the company or decision makers that may tie in to your product or service could be very helpful. The more information you have on the company the better prepared you will be to speak with someone live on the phone.

The cold call isn't just cold for the decision makers. During a cold call the decision makers have a brief moment before they answer when they are mentally aware they're about to be speaking with someone. Because of that they already have an advantage over the sales person calling them. As cold callers we have no idea who is going to answer our calls, or who is going to be like most decision makers and send us to voicemail. That's why it's really important to get yourself mentally ready on every dial. You should feel disappointed if they don't answer. If you feel relief when you hear their voicemail pick up you need to change that. You can work on it by controlling what you're thinking, as the phone is ringing actually say things to yourself like "Pick Up the Phone, man". If their voicemail picks up get mad about it, say to yourself "crap" or "next time you'll talk to me". It may sound crazy but we chose to be in a profession where we call people who seriously don't want to talk to us. I'd say crazy waived bye-bye to us in the mirror a long time ago. You know the saying 'you are what you eat'? A few others and I believe 'you are what you think'. Positive thinking in work and life might make a bigger difference than you could ever imagine.

I treat cold calling a lot like I'm playing a sport. Every dial to me is like a free throw or an at bat in baseball. I know not everybody is an athlete but if you've chose to work in the profession of sales that means you're probably pretty competitive. So whatever you do that makes you compete, treat cold calling like that. As part of my cold calling routine I like to call in sessions and I will usually make my cold calls between 4pm to 5pm. I've found that decision makers are far more receptive to productive conversations at this time of the day. My next ideal time of the day to make cold calls is at the decision maker's lunch time. If for some reason I'm calling a few different time zones then that can work out to be a two hour calling session.

Prior to a call session (basically the entire day) I've prepared my call list. I have all the information I need on the companies and contacts to make my initial contact. I make my calls from my cellphone while standing with earbuds and move from one call to the next inputting pertinent info into my CRM (I use Zoho). Between calls I listen to Pandora as it automatically comes back on after I hang up each dial, the music keeps me calm and happy. It's like having a nice friend in my corner while I'm dealing with some mean people for an hour or two. Before each dial I also take in a brief review of the company and contact information. If I'm going to leave a voicemail I'll review it and maybe even practice it. Along with Zoho, I also like to keep open the contact's LinkedIn and maybe the company's website for quick access in case the decision maker picks up.

During the call session I move from call to call in this manner, sometimes I can make up to 30 or more dials in an hour. The number of calls I'm able to make really depends on how many good prospects I'm pursuing at the time, how many decision makers I actually speak with, and how many voicemails I leave. Activity and volume certainly play into your overall success as a sales person. But the quality of what you do will affect your results far more than anything else. Make sure you're calling on the right companies and the right contacts. I'm sure that you know spending your time calling on businesses that are not a good fit for your product or service is a waste of time that you can't afford. If you're doing silly things like calling fifteen people at one company in order to meet your required call volume, sales may not be the right gig for you. Successful sales people make cold calls for no other reason than to sell new business and acquire more customers.

9

Getting Decision Makers to

Answer the Phone

As I mentioned earlier in the book I had the experience of being a SMB owner called on by hundreds of sales reps over the course of 10 years. At first it was interesting and almost fun because I've spent so much time in my career cold calling. But just like other decision makers it became overwhelming and it was easier for me to not pick up the phone. However, I did give some sales people a chance and I can only remember one reason for doing that. It was because I appreciated the persistence of that particular sales representative. Don't get me wrong if a sales rep harassed me with calls every other day or left several voice messages, I wouldn't give them the time of day. Partly because I was annoyed but mostly because I understood they wouldn't keep up this level of harassment. Their approach was predictable and I knew that eventually they would quit calling and I wouldn't hear from them again for a year or ever. This was just my personal experience being on the other end of cold calls. I think it's important to understand that all the decision makers we're calling are different and we need to be ready to treat them accordingly.

My cold calling approach to get a decision maker to answer the phone may seem simple, but this is a proven method that has worked over two decades for me and many other successful sales people. The key to the approach is patience and being ready at a moment's notice to turn the tide with a conversation. Tragically, it's possible that the products or services that we are selling may not be crucial to this decision maker at this very moment. Trying to get them to react to us in an impatient time frame is only going to turn them off. Cold calling etiquette 101, don't call decision makers too frequently. With my approach if I don't connect in my first handful of touches I'm going to be committed to this effort for the long haul. By only periodically giving a decision maker a call it shows them that I'm not going to stop calling until there is a conversation. It also lets them know that I'm a professional and I'm not going to harass them during this process.

Before we get into the details of my approach let's talk about the best time of day to call a decision maker. Throughout my career my most successful time of the day to call has been without question between 4pm to 5pm in the prospect's time zone. At this time of day most decision makers have wrapped up their meetings and are probably finishing up some things before going home. Their mood may be better because the day is almost over but most importantly they may actually have a few minutes to absorb your message. I'm not saying this is the only time of the day to call but I've found without a doubt it to be the most effective. If you're trying to explain more technical concepts, calling later in the day around this time frame is especially necessary. I've found that other good times of the day to reach decision makers are during the prospects lunch time or before 9:30am, that's of course if you're the early morning type. First thing in the business day is also a great time to leave voicemails but as far as conversations, you'll usually only catch other early birds. Many decision makers aren't going to answer their phones earlier in the morning because they could be preparing for meetings or something else that's coming up in their day. Or maybe they're like me and prefer not to have conversations in the early morning hours. If you're currently calling decision makers in the mid-morning or mid-afternoon hours, then you're calling them at exactly the best time to not reach them. Decision makers are often times in meetings during these mid-morning and mid-afternoon segments of the day. Oddly enough, during my career these were the times of the day when I would see most sales representatives making cold calls.

Back to my approach, sorry I hate to use the word cadence. I guess I associate it with the modern 'react to me right now' strategy. Anyway, I prefer the term approach and I'll often call it my approach but I'm sure many other sales reps in the world have logically come to a similar method. Now that we've discussed time of day to call let's talk about some of the approach details. My approach isn't an exact sequence of events but it always starts out the same with me giving the decision maker a couple of dials over the first two weeks. I usually make these first calls in the 4pm to 5pm timeframe, typically on a Tuesday or Wednesday. In these first few calls I'm primarily hoping to catch the decision maker in a conversation before they know anything about me or my company. I'm also making these dials so I can understand the lay of the land. I want to know if there is a gatekeeper, I want to hear the decision maker's voicemail, and any other pertinent information that I can gather just by making a few dials.

The day of the week in which you make cold calls doesn't really matter too much because decision makers all have different routines and quirks. Other than calling Monday morning or late Friday afternoon I think decision makers are going to pick up that phone based on a whim. Don't limit yourself by only calling on Tuesdays because you had a really good cold call on Tuesday a few years ago. Understand that you aren't the person you're calling and thus you have no idea where they are, what mood they're in, or if they're going to pick up your call. But if you approach them in a way that doesn't piss them off they might just take your call someday and give you a chance to turn the tide.

Okay, back to the steps of my approach. Assuming I don't get a hold of the decision maker in the first two dials over the first two weeks (which is usually the case). At this point I will most often use a tactic I call **quick chat.** The point or objective of this tactic is to make the decision maker feel like I just want to have a short conversation to make sure they're aware of something. I'll usually give quick chat a try a few weeks after my second dial. Here is how it works, before I make my next dial during that morning I will send the decision maker an email letting them vaguely know why I'm trying to reach them. What is written in the email is very important because remember we don't want to give the decision maker too much information so they can eliminate us altogether. We also don't want our email to be so short and cryptic that it comes off as spam. The primary objective of the email is make them feel like there is some information that we have they may want to know about, it can be especially effective if you can mention one of their competitors in this email. Here is a sample of a Quick Chat email:

Decision Maker,

Friendly email to let you know that I'll be trying to reach you to share some information on…

> …how your company can save a billion dollars. Similar to what happened for ABC Company (their competitor) last year.

> …how your company can grow your revenues. Similar to what DEF company was able to achieve in North America.

> …how your company can significantly decrease waste in the manufacturing operation. Most companies in your industry are unaware of this technology.

I just need a few minutes to explain.

Best regards,

Sales Rep Just Talk to Me

The most important aspect of the email is the trigger that gets them interested in knowing more about what you have to say. Every company and sales situation will have its own triggers and if you're having trouble writing this sentence it may be a great time to get with sales rep Dave and ask him some really good questions.

Please keep in mind you're only sending the quick chat email in order to get them to have a conversation with you. The last thing you want to do is load the email with information about why your company is so awesome. If you can get the decision maker to answer the phone a verbal conversation will give you a much better chance of making sure they understand your company's true value proposition in the way you want them to see it. If you happen to be aligning on timing, don't worry because they'll understand enough about your company from this email to respond to you. When aligning on timing a response from the decision maker or a member of their team will usually come back almost instantly.

In order to complete quick chat, later that day I'll give the decision maker a call. I don't know the exact percentage of decision makers that pick up with this strategy but I can tell you that I'm not at all surprised when they do. And if I was able to mention one of their main competitors in the email, I'm a little surprised sometimes when they don't pick up.

In lieu of quick chat at this stage sometimes I'll reverse things and I'll leave a voicemail followed up with an email, I call this **opportunity knocks**. Similar to the quick chat email, I don't give them too much information in the voicemail. I tell them who I am and my company name and I also reference a possible opportunity. I'm not really leaving this message because of the content. As sales people we have no idea if our voicemails will even be listened to by the decision maker, most are not. I'm leaving the voicemail because I want the decision maker to hear my voice. I want them to understand that if we speak we're going to have a professional conversation. If you're not good at leaving voicemails then you need to practice. The better your voicemail sounds the more likely a decision maker will be to pick up your call.

I keep all my voicemails short, around thirty to forty seconds depending on what I'm saying. I've been around sales people who leave longer voicemails and they make it work but it better be dang good if it's going to be a whole minute long. In order to leave the perfect voicemail I'll prerecord them using Zoho. It's important for me that I really nail it when I deliver this message. I want the decision maker to know they're dealing with a professional. My voicemails are always followed up with an email to make sure I'm connecting if there happens to be an alignment of timing. A follow up email to any voicemail is nice because then the decision maker doesn't have to write anything down. I think most of them appreciate that and they'll even expect it in some cases. I don't leave my phone number in my voicemails. I just let the decision maker know I'll be sending an email suggesting a time for us to speak.

Sample Opportunity Knocks Voicemail:

Hi Doug, this is Matt Wanty with MyCompany. Recently researching your company we noticed that you're currently not selling your products in Europe. I'm wondering if this is an opportunity that is being considered. MyCompany has helped other retailers like blah, blah, and blah successfully expand into this and other markets. Doug, I'll email you and suggest a time for us to speak. Thanks for your time, have a great day.

The opportunity knocks' email is a follow up to the voicemail and like everything else the email should be short. It should reiterate the opportunity and ask for a specific time to speak with the decision maker.

Sample Opportunity Knocks email:

Doug,

My recent message asked about a possible opportunity to sell your products to a broader market.

In a few minutes I could explain how ABC Company achieved a 25% increase in sales by expanding in Europe.

Would Thursday, April 15th @ 9a ET work for a brief conversation?

Sincerely,

Good Info Sales Person

If my third attempt at a conversation doesn't succeed than I will likely repeat step 3 once more by flip flopping tactics quick chat and opportunity knocks. If I used opportunity knocks then I'll try quick chat and vice versa. I'll typically wait three to four weeks after step 3 before I'll try to use the other tactic. However, I may decide to skip that all together and put this decision maker directly into my Must Reach category. Must Reach means I've decided that until this decision maker understands what my company does, it's my job to pursue them via the phone. This decision maker has officially become a permanent target for me to speak with and I'm digging in for the long haul.

As a general rule I don't like leaving any more than two voicemails but I'll usually only leave one. The decision makers we're calling on are not stupid. Most of them hate voicemails because they can become a pain to check when you have so many sales people calling you. All the voices begin to sound the same and the content of messages seems so self-serving. It can become especially annoying when the decision maker is trying to find an important message from their boss or a client and they have to scan thru a lot of voicemails from sales reps. Decision makers may not always check their voicemail every day. They may be traveling or other pressing matters may be occupying their time. Having two messages on a decision maker's voicemail when they check it could put you in a category that as sales people we never want to be in. When the busy decision maker finally gets a chance to check their voicemail, they're not just listening to one message from you that they find annoying but now they're hearing your lovely voice twice. It is always best to space out your voicemails at least a few weeks at a time to avoid this being you.

If I decided to skip the fourth step and take this decision maker right to Must Reach, then I will still send a second email or just resend my first email. This is important because since decision makers are usually busy it's possible the first email fell through the cracks. If they had considered responding to your first email, then there is a really good chance they will respond to a 2nd email even if things haven't slowed down for them. Otherwise, I'd stay away from sending more than two emails as well. Voicemails and emails could give the decision maker information that in their mind is a reason they don't need to speak with us.

Okay, so after we've tried our emails and voicemails without success this decision maker is now officially a Must Reach contact. Since they haven't taken the time to reject me I'm going to become a regular addition to their caller ID. It's very important that as sales people the phone you are calling from clearly shows your company's name when calling prospects. If our CompanyName shows up on the decision maker's caller ID then every dial we make is an official touch or contact. If your phone call shows up as some random cell number, then they won't have any idea it was you or your company. Some wireless service providers, such as Verizon, allow you to customize your phone's caller ID name. I like to think that every time the decision maker sees my company's name we're one step closer to a conversation. Optimistically hopeful, yes I am. At this point in my approach the decision maker visually seeing my company's name on their caller ID is the only tool in my toolbox. Whether they see my company name as I'm calling or later on when they're scrolling through their missed calls it doesn't matter. For at least the next six months I'll only be dialing and I won't be sending any emails or leaving any voicemails. As they keep seeing my company name that will at least become more familiar to them over time.

By periodically calling over the next 6 months I'm hoping to catch the decision maker at that right time when they're willing to have a conversation. Periodically means don't call them too often and put them on the defensive. It's okay to call a decision maker once a week but that's pretty predictable so you don't want to do that. Over the six months I mix it up, I start out by calling once a week and at other points I'll take a few weeks or a month off between calls. A few times I'll try giving them a call in the morning and another in the afternoon on the same day, I call this **two times** – it's a movie reference. After three or four months into the process I will try calling them three days in a row, I call this

pretty please - IDK, no reference. Two times and pretty please are effective tactics at pushing decision makers to pick up the phone in order to get us to stop calling them. When one of these strategies works for you (and they will) understand the decision maker may answer the phone a little hotter and bothered than normal. Use your own discretion with these strategies and monikers but always lean on the side of not trying to annoy the person you're calling, well at least not too much. Don't be afraid to be creative and try new things with stubborn decision makers. If you happen to come up with any calling tactics that are worth sharing you have my email address, homie.

By approaching decision makers in this manner we are playing the odds and trying to catch them at that right moment. It's important to understand there is a very real chance that over that six month period you will actually get them on the phone. I can't give you an exact percentage but I can tell you I've reached decision makers in my Must Reach category at every point of the process. So be ready, but be patient, but be ready ☺. There are some other little things I do in order to get decision makers to pick up the phone. Once in a great while I'll make calls from my personal cell phone so my company's name doesn't show on the caller ID. Sometimes decision makers will pick up thinking I'm somebody else. If the decision maker you are trying to reach resides in a city where you happen to know a lot of events are going on in a certain month, don't call them that month. Do anything you can to seem more considerate than the other sales people biding for their chance at a conversation. In the end these little things might put you in a handful more conversations in a week, a month, or a year depending on your normal connect rate. If you become a good cold caller, even just a few more conversations could result in a significant increase in your annual sales numbers and income.

The largest sale of my career, it took me right around six months to get the Vice President of Finance at this Fortune 500 Company to pick up his phone. After six months of dialing, our first conversation went something like this: He picked up the phone with a really gruff "This is Rick". I said "Hi Rick, this is Matt Wanty from Airborne Express". He interrupted before I could say anything else and even more gruffly said "What do you need?" I instantly fired back asking with concern "Rick, is this a bad time?", Rick said "Yes, I was just headed out for the day" and I said "I'll try to catch you at better time", click I hung up and no other words were spoken. It was my cold calling instinct to react this way, his voice was way too rough and we weren't going to have the conversation I needed. It had been six months of calling him but I knew instantly I had to let the conversation go. I may have never gotten Rick back on the phone but when it's not right it's not right. Rick fortunately answered my call the very next week, I was able to turn the tide and we scheduled a meeting. Within six weeks of that first meeting Rick and I were flying around the country implementing our new multi-million dollar relationship. It was a huge deal, the agreement initiated a meeting between our two Fortune 500 CEOs just a few months later. I was flying high, the end result of my cold calling effort was as good as it can possibly get.

Wrapping up the details of my approach, so six months has gone by and using my tactics I have periodically called this decision maker and they've never answered my call. It doesn't have to be exactly six months and in many cases I will push it a few more months if I feel like it. Even though the decision maker was unresponsive, I have decided this is a good prospect for my company and I'm going to continually pursue them. Remember, I haven't turned this person off to my company yet, well at least they haven't expressed that to me. Based on the information I provided to this decision maker they shouldn't have been able to form too much of an opinion of my company and eliminate me all together. I still need to speak with them in order for them to understand my company's true value proposition and thus they'll remain a Must Reach contact for me. As you continuously prospect the number of decision makers you've labeled as Must Reach should continue to grow. Maintaining a Must Reach list gives sales people an identified group in which to continuously attempt to cold call. This gives us a real opportunity to connect in conversations with decision makers through a long term effort.

Since my first full approach to reach this decision maker has finished unsuccessful it is time for me to take two or three months off and restart again at a later date TBD. But before I begin my next approach I will review my initial research and refresh any new findings. I'm going to check for other contacts at the company that may be worth pursuing; maybe a new player has joined the organization. I may even decide to call higher up the food chain at the C-level. The way I look at it this decision maker didn't take the time to speak with me and their company has no idea what we can do for them. The final thing I'm going to do before I start a fresh approach is fine tune my messaging. I'll include anything that may be new or maybe I'll try to convey my message in a different way. After a few months of letting this decision maker rest it will be time to pursue them and their company all over again. They simply need to know what my company can do for them.

Does my approach work every time to get a decision maker into a conversation? It does not, but we all know there isn't a sales or cold calling methodology that will get every decision maker to pick up their phone, not even close. My approach has allowed me to speak to significantly more decision makers than my colleagues at every stop of my career for two simple reasons; I never give up and I don't get myself eliminated by providing too much information. As an outbound sales person everything I do is geared toward creating a conversation with the decision maker. It isn't going to happen with every prospect but I continue to call knowing that I will get some opportunities to turn the tide. This is normally the part where the author tells you that they nail every conversation. Those people are full of crap. I fail on cold calls just like everybody else. Fortunately, with years of experience I do succeed in most conversations with decision makers and you can too. Everything I know about turning the tide with a conversation is in the next chapters.

10

The Call – Seizing the Opportunity

Before we get into the actual call it's important that we understand a little bit about why this person took our call in the first place. You may not realize it but there are actually reasons why decision makers pick up our disrupting cold calls. Having a general understanding of why they answered your call can go a long way in helping you effectively communicate with this person. One of the most common reasons decision makers pick up the phone is that they simply want to get sales people to stop calling them. It could also be because you're a lucky cat and you're calling when it's really good timing, or they've mistaken your phone number for someone else, or they're doing their job that day and talking with prospective vendors. At some point during the conversation you may realize why they picked up the phone and you can try to use that information in your favor. It's also important to understand that once the decision maker has picked up your call the first thing they probably want to know is what your company provides. They want to know this so they can quickly eliminate you as a possible vendor and get back to whatever it was they were doing before you interrupted them.

Okay, so the decision maker has finally picked up one of your cold calls and its go time. It all starts when you hear the clicking sound that lets you know that someone is going to be on the other end of the line. In a moment a guarded person is going to say in a less than happy voice, "this is Doug". Don't let the anger or agitation in their voice dissuade you from the task at hand. Remember, this person knows nothing about your company's true value proposition and it's your chance to tell them. Of course he or she is agitated because of one or many of the things mentioned in chapter 6. Before we can get to our true value proposition we'll need to get this cowboy off their high horse. I've found it's always best to keep the focus on them while we try to do this. The first few sentences that you're going to spout out to this impatient person need to be really good. Not just the content of what you say but the way in which you say it. You should know these sentences like the back of your iPhone and be able to say them with seeming confidence at a moment's notice, under any circumstances.

My intro usually goes something like these samples:

> Hi Doug, how you doing, this is Matt Wanty with MyCompany. I've been reaching out to in regards to your website, prospectname.com, I'm trying to find out if you're considering a version of the site to support your European operations?

> Hi Doug, how you doing, this is Matt Wanty with MyCompany. I'm reaching out to you in regards to your company's office equipment. I'm trying find out if you were aware of alternative type of office furniture on the market?

> Hi Doug, good afternoon, this is Matt Wanty with MyCompany. I'm reaching out to you in regards to your company's security. I'm trying you find out if your company is considering (something they're missing).

> Hi Alan, good afternoon, this is Eric Singer with Landmark. I'm calling you in regards to your firm's litigation services. I'm trying you find out if you or your partners were aware of a new document scanning technology?

> Hi Billy, good morning, this is Sharon Manny with Marketing Company. I'm calling you in regards to your company's marketing plan. I was wondering if

you were aware of a new tech tool that allows you to (do something really awesome)?

The first words and sentences we speak on a cold call give the decision maker the opportunity to measure us up. They're determining whether or not it's even worth their time to listen to more. You and I both know that some of these decision makers will just hang up the phone on sales people if they don't like what we're saying. Don't let them do that, be ready every time and nail these first few sentences. Let that decision maker know they are speaking with a highly professional sales representative. They'll take you and your message a lot more seriously if you can deliver your opening statement like Fluffy tells a joke. Clarification, in my intro I don't actually ask them how are they doing. I just say the words "how you doing" as an extended greeting. If you ask them that question you're going to create an awkward moment. They don't know you so you don't want to ask them personal questions like how they're doing, that can be weird.

As part of our opening statement we're going to give these decision makers what they want, well sort of. Our first sentences should let them know generally what topic we're calling about without letting them eliminate our company altogether. My statement "I'm reaching out to you about your website". With that the decision maker has a general idea about why I'm calling but not enough information to hang up the phone. By not giving the decision maker too much information right away they can't quickly say they're not involved and you should call somebody else.

I'm sure you noticed I ended my intro statement with a question for the decision maker. Yes, this was indeed a closed-ended question. Apparently, some of the trendy sales teachings being stolen around are focused on asking open-ended questions when calling prospects. I believe the concept of asking open-ended questions is to get the decision maker talking more umm, open-endedly. Well, I'm from the real world of cold calling and I couldn't disagree with this concept more. I specifically want the first question that I ask a decision maker to be closed-ended because this gives them only one of two ways to respond. Of course I'll be ready with a response for either answer they give me.

Making a point to ask open-ended questions on a cold call could take the conversation into several different directions that we're possibly not ready to handle. It could also really annoy the decision maker. There's a time to ask questions that get decision makers talking freely but it's definitely not at the early stages of a cold call. On a cold call we're trying to get a next step and in order to do that we need the decision maker to understand the value our company can offer. We have to control the conversation throughout the call to make sure we get the opportunity to properly convey our true value proposition. The first scheduled sales meeting is a great setting to ask open-ended questions so you can begin to tailor your offering around the prospect's specific needs.

Always keep in mind when creating your opening statement that we're engaging in a conversation with someone who doesn't want to be speaking with us. The best way that I know to handle that is by making it all about them. I'm calling about **your** website to see if **you** are considering something. Even though it's seemingly about them doesn't mean the decision maker won't derive what my company does from those few sentences. We want them to do that and we want them to talk to us about it. Where ever their brain takes them after our opening lines, it's good because they're thinking about our company and how it relates to them. However, at this point they're still very much angling to get cold callers off the phone but they also want to satisfy the matter so you don't call them back again. This is our chance cold calling warriors; we can't let them satisfy the matter.

After you perfectly deliver your opening statement they'll probably still answer your question by saying, "we already have that" or "we don't need that". The next chapter covers a specific strategy that I use to handle this type of general and absolute objection. If the decision maker gives an objection that's more specific to your company or your industry then you should already have some insight from your training on how to handle those common objections. For example, a hosting company may receive an objection because of the specific type of servers they use for their data warehouses. They will have faced this objection numerous times and will know exactly the best way to respond or they wouldn't be in business. It's very important that you master this type of specific information about your company and market in order to become a great cold caller.

During a cold call the point of the decision maker's first objection is a pivotal spot. In this moment we want our response to get the other end of the line to start digging deeper. We want them to start realizing maybe they don't have all the information, maybe listening to what another vendor has to say could be beneficial to them and their company. If you can provide a solid answer to their first objection and then turn that into another question, this cold call may now be headed in the direction you want. If you don't respond well to this first objection you may get a more resounding no and you'll have to concede. A couple other little things you should keep in mind during a cold call conversation: Anytime the decision maker is talking make sure they finish before you respond. If you both start talking at the same time, which can happen in any conversation, make sure to insist they speak first. Always remember when the going gets rough on a cold call, education trumps objections and I'll explain what that's all about in the next chapter.

11

Education Trumps Objections

What I mean by 'education trumps objections' is that even if a decision maker comes to the conclusion that their business has no need for your product or service and thus no need to continue talking to you, if in that very moment of the conversation you can begin to teach this person something new, they'll continue to listen to what you have to say. People are naturally inquisitive and a person in the position of decision maker usually doesn't like it when there is important information they possibly don't know. If you can take them from a defensive buyer state to an educational student state, you'll be in a great position to effectively convey your company's true value proposition and get a next step. Much easier said than done I know but if you master this technique of handling objections you will be a more effective cold caller then you ever thought possible.

When facing absolute objections during a cold call, such as "no we don't need that" or "we already have that", this is when I revert to questions that lead to education. For example:

> Decision maker says "we already handle that in house", I respond "did you know there is a much cheaper or more efficient way to do this...?"

> Decision maker says "We already use a company called Big Losers for that." My response "Are you aware you can save money by doing it this way? I'm not sure Big Losers has the equipment to do that."

> Decision maker says "We don't need your help" My response "I'm glad to hear things are going well but did you know we helped CrushingYou Co. grow 10% last year?"

> Decision maker says "That decision is handled at a lower level." My response "I understand someone else manages the vendor but what I'm calling to discuss is a little bigger picture. Did you know your company could do this cool thing?"

> Decision maker says "I heard your company provides poor service." My response "We were a start up at one point but I can tell you nowadays we provide a

really strong service for our clients. Do you know customer reference?"

There can come a point in any cold call where the decision maker is digging in hard and making their final bid to get you off the phone. When decision makers are trying to put me on what I call the 'cold calling ropes', I like to use last stand statements like this:

Most companies don't know that this service or product is even available and it may be something you want to know more about.

Customer (reference customer) had that same feeling before they learned more about our efficient approach.

Customer (reference customer) decided to take a deeper look and found better solutions.

It's my job to make sure that you are aware of what my company does, most companies have no idea what we offer is even available.

Manipulation is a powerful and appropriate tool in cold calling, but you have to use it wisely. Statements that make the decision maker feel like they're possibly missing something can put you in a great position to convey your company's true value proposition. But they must be delivered in a way that doesn't make you seem like a jerk. Whether you get a next step or not, if you're able to covey your company's true value proposition to a decision maker on a cold call, you did a really good job. If you're able to the turn the tide and secure a next step, be especially proud because you have just defied the laws of timing and that takes a lot of skill.

12

Next Steps Add Up

As sales professionals we live in the world of next steps. Our job is to keep the ball rolling with accounts and always keep the possibility of our two companies doing business alive. Sometimes decision makers and their companies are not in a position to buy and it can be for a number of different reasons. There could be a spending freeze at the company, or an impending merger, or new leadership could be coming on board in the near future. As sales people we have no control over bigger picture factors like these. I'm from the experience that decision makers buy exactly when they're ready to buy. As sales people we can certainly influence timelines by providing solutions that solve large problems or save our customers lots of money. The bigger the internal win for our decision maker the greater the motivation for change.

However, I think it's important to always keep in mind that sometimes bigger business forces can be preventing or delaying our sales. When pursuing decision makers for action it is always best to keep in mind that they may have bigger fish to fry at the moment. They may not always tell you that and it's better to not make them by over chasing. As long as you're selling at the right level you can afford to be patient with your decision makers. Bigger projects or issues can always come down from the C-level and business plans can be altered or pushed out. As sales people we have to respect our decision maker's timelines and protect them from impatient harassment. Business strategies that try to get decision makers to speed up their purchasing timelines can come off as selfish or desperate.

The more next steps we're able to garner while cold calling the bigger our eventual sales funnels and pipelines. The more times we're able to share our company's true value proposition the greater our chances for long term success and potential income. In any market or industry it can take at least a year or two for a sales rep to start realizing the fruits of their labor, in some cases even longer. It's always important to be looking at the bigger picture of your efforts and its okay to be patient in outbound sales if that's what you feel is best with that prospect. The decision makers you're pursuing will appreciate your patience and respect you more for it.

13

Communication

When it's all said and done a cold call is just a conversation between two people. As sales pros it's our job to make sure the communication is on point as best we can. I've shared my tactics on handling tough decision makers and objections, but there are more communication things I've learned over the years that I'm not qualified to share in this book. Around 15 years ago I read one of the most important books of my life called 'How to Communicate' by Matthew McKay. At the time I was trying to improve my communication skills and I had been recommended the author. I put the lessons of this book into action in my life and I fundamentally changed the way I communicated forever. As sales people in order to be successful we MUST be good communicators. After I absorbed the teachings of 'How to Communicate' my life and sales career became significantly better. The concepts in the book may seem simple but when you start to compare them to how you're actually communicating, you may quickly realize that you have some work to do. That was at least my experience.

This chapter on communication is a little short so I guess it's as good a place as any for my spiel on mock cold calling. Do it! Seriously though, I spent a lot of time mock cold calling in my first five or so years in sales. Obviously a mock cold call means a fake cold call between two people from the same company. It's a really important exercise if you want to become a highly skilled cold caller. It's the equivalent of a flight simulator for a pilot, a dress rehearsal for actors, or a testing lab for scientists and engineers. This is live practice that can be done between a sales rep and a sales trainer or manager, or two sales reps can also perform mock cold calls on their own. One important thing to keep in mind when you're practicing mock cold calls, keep it realistic. Use objections that sales people from your company could actually hear from a decision maker. There seems to be an odd effect with mock cold calling where sales reps and even managers take the conversation down roads never traveled. Keep your mock cold calling simple and make sure you're giving each other real objections. One of the great things about mock cold calling is that both ends of the line are learning. Playing the role of buyer gives sales people and even trainers and managers a little perspective as to what it's like to be a decision maker on the other end of a cold call.

14

Time is On Your Side

While attending one of Airborne Express' corporate sales trainings (boot-camp), the trainer Shannon McGinnis made a small group of fellas in the class stand up and sing the song, 'Time is On Your Side'. It was really early in the morning and a big night out before in the small Ohio town had us all a little hungover. As we were grudgingly standing up I remember thinking this is going to be really bad. We actually sounded pretty good but that's not the point I'm trying to make here. Within just a few seconds of singing the song I connected with Shannon's message. Maybe we all did and that's why we didn't kill anybody's ears that morning. As sales people we are in an occupation where numerous hours of target account pursuit can result in absolutely nothing. As cold callers we can make hundreds of dials to only reach a few of the people we're calling. The reality for us Einstein's that chose this 'what have you done for me lately' profession is that a lot of our time goes wasted. We have to accept this as sales people and understand we're not going to speak with every decision maker or land every account. This particular sales training moment obviously stuck with me over the years and I think it's really important for every sales person to always remember, time really is on your side. No matter what happens with each cold call or target account, we'll be more experienced and better prepared to sell the next one.

Promise from the Author:

As I was writing this book I would periodically read on-line reviews for the other sales training and cold calling books on the market. Much like my sales process, I did this because I wanted to know as much as I could about my prospective customer. The intelligence I gathered on the book's target market was great but I also learned a lot about on-line book reviews in the process. It seems the only reviews that you can even be certain are real are the negative ones. Many of the positive reviews for the more popular sales training books seemed fake to me. I'm not trying to start anything I'm just calling it like I see it. In my opinion some of the reviews read as if the reviewer was writing a summary of the book straight from the author's mouth, IDK.

Here is my promise to anyone who cares; you will never see a fake review for anything I create in my life ever, period. Whether I create a book, a company, or a batch of Cuban coffee, all the reviews will be completely REAL, I promise. If this book helps a sales representative become a better cold caller and thus, improve their financial situation, all I could hope for is a review that said "best 10 bucks I ever spent". That's real to me.

Other Books to Check Out:

I grew up in sales with these books

'Strategic Sales' – Authors: Robert B. Miller, Stephen E. Heiman, and Tad Tuleja.

'Conceptual Selling' – Authors: Robert B. Miller, Stephen E. Heiman, and Tad Tuleja.

I grew up in life with these books

'How to Communicate' – Authors: Martha Davis, Matthew McKay, and Patrick Fanning.

'A Guide to a Rational Living' – Authors: Albert Ellis and Robert A. Harper (anxiety and nerves and so much more)

~ Notes ~

~ Notes ~

~ Notes ~

~ Notes ~

~ Notes ~

~ Notes ~

~ Notes ~

~ Notes ~